St. Paul's Anglican Churchyard J - N

The Grave Whisperer

Angeline Gallant

Published by Angeline Gallant, 2022.

ST. PAUL'S ANGLICAN CHURCHYARD J - N

First edition. September 10, 2022.

ISBN: 979-8215524299

Written by Angeline Gallant.

Also by Angeline Gallant

A Dragon's Diary
Dreaming of Dragons

Blood and Spirit Saga
The Rising Wind

Calling Her Heart
Whisper of the Heart
Calling Her Heart Volumes 1 & 2: A Small Town Romance
Collection
No Turning Back
Calling Her Heart volumes 3 & 4
Forsake Me Not
Hear My Cry

FORGET ME NOT
Victoria, Ontario's Babies 1894 - 1895

Guardian of the Heart
Fallen Petals

Keeper Of Secrets
A Lady's Secret

Kingston's Love Chronicles
Springtime Promises

Midnight's Awakening
Heart of the Storm
Walking Through The Storm
Walking Through The Storm
Fighting the Storm
Call Me Cursed
Heart of the Storm

Secrets of the Underworld
Deklan's Dragons

Tell My Story Collection
Tell My Story: Germany 1851
Tell My Story: England 1852

Whispers From The Garrison Church

The Dervock Legacy
Echoes of Dervock

The Grave Whisperer
German Prisoners of War in Canada
Cataraqui United Church Cemetery
Whispers of Kingston
Wedding Bells in Kingston, Ontario, Canada 1923
St. Paul's Anglican Churchyard A-B
St. Paul's Anglican Churchyard C-D
St. Paul's Anglican Churchyard E - F
St. Paul's Anglican Churchyard, Kingston, Ontario, Canada G - H
St. Paul's Anglican Churchyard J - N
St. Paul's Anglican Churchyard, Kingston, Ontario, Canada O - R
St. Paul's Anglican Churchyard, Kingston, Ontario, Canada S - T
St. Paul's Anglican Churchyard, Kingston, Ontario T - Z
Small Graveyards & Burial Grounds: Kingston, Ontario, Canada
Cataraqui United Church Cemetery 1
Cataraqui United Church Cemetery 2
Cataraqui United Church Cemetary 3
Cataraqui United Church Cemetery 4
Cataraqui United Church Cemetery 5
Beth Israel Cemetery
Cataraqui United Church Cemetery 6
Beneath the Surface: Echoes from Beth Israel Cemetery
Grave Tales: Discovering the Lives of Beth Israel
Whispers Beneath St. Paul's

The Timeless Veil
Eternal Devotion

The Wolf Whisperer Series
Captured Heart
Fate's Legacy
Mohawk Valley
Cry of a Warrior
Wolf Whisperer volumes 1 & 2
Endless White
The Wolf Whisperer volumes 1 & 2

Timeless
The Time Keeper's Sanctuary

Timeless Whispers of Dervock Saga
Secrets of Dervock

Standalone
Winds of Change vol 1-3

Watch for more at https://www.goodreads.com/author/show/ 19703964.Angeline_Gallant.

Table of Contents

WILLIAM JACKSON[1]

William passed away in 1818 and was buried in Kingston, Frontenac, Upper Canada, British Colonial America. A church was built over his grave.

NICHOLAS JAMES[2]

Nicholas was buried on October 22, 1807 in Kingston, Frontenac, Upper Canada, British Colonial America. A church was built over his grave.

MARY JELLEY[3]

Mary was buried on November 29, 1806 in Kingston, Frontenac, Upper Canada, British Colonial America. A church was built over her grave.

MARGARET JOHNSON[4]

Margaret was buried on March 20, 1802 in Kingston, Frontenac, Upper Canada, British Colonial America. A church was built over her grave.

MARY DEGONWADONTI (BRANT) JOHNSON[5]

(*She is famous. Please check out the footnote for further information*) "Molly" was born on April 13, 1736 in New York.

She was six years old when her father passed away in 1743.

Molly was 16 years old when she entered into a common-law marriage with Sir. William Johnson in 1752.

She was 38 years old when her husband passed away in 1774.

Molly was 42 years old when her mother passed away in 1779.

She was 60 years old when she passed away on April 16, 1796.

WILLIAM JOHNSON[6]

William was only a child when he was buried on February 2, 1796 in Kingston, Frontenac, Upper Canada, British Colonial America. A church was built over his grave.

WILLIAM JOHNSON[7]

William was buried on December 2, 1805 in Kingston, Frontenac, Upper Canada, British Colonial America. A church was built over his grave.

CHILLIAN JONES[8]

They were buried in Kingston, Ontario. Nothing else is currently known. A church was built over the grave.

JAMES JONES[9]

James was a boatswain when he was buried on May 24, 1796 in Kingston, Frontenac, Upper Canada, British Colonial America. A church was built over his grave.

MARY (STUART) JONES[10]

Mary was born on May 19, 1785 in Kingston, Frontenac, Upper Canada, British Colonial America.

She was less than a year old when the Shay's Rebellion took place in 1786.

Mary was five years old when the first parliament of Upper Canada assembled on September 17, 1791.

She was 22 years old when she married Hon. Charles Jones, Esq. on June 8, 1807 in Elizabethtown-Kitley, Ontario.

Mary was 26 years old when her father passed away in 1811.

She was 27 years old when the War of 1812 took place. Mary passed away on October 25th and was buried in Kingston on October 27th.

RICHARD JONES[11]

Richard was a child when he passed away in 1813. A church was built over his grave.

PETER KANTZ[12]

Peter was buried on October 12, 1801 in Kingston, Frontenac, Upper Canada, British Colonial America. A church was built over his grave.

JOHN KAYTON[13]

John was buried on January 8, 1795 in Kingston, Frontenac, Upper Canada, British Colonial America. A church was built over his grave.

ANN KEITH[14]

Ann passed away in 1813 and was buried in Kingston, Frontenac, Upper Canada, British Colonial America. A church was built over her grave.

CATHERINE ELIZABETH KILLALY[15]

Catherine was born in 1840.

She was a year old when she passed away on July 21, 1841. She was buried in Kingston, Frontenac, Canada West, British Colonial America. Her grave is located beneath the parish hall of a church that was built over her grave.

JOHN KINDLE[16]

John passed away in 1822. A church was built over his grave in Kingston, Ontario.

MARY KIRBY[17]

Mary was born in 1783.

She was eight years old when the first parliament of Upper Canada assembled on September 17, 1791.

Mary was 54 years old when she passed away on January 17, 1837. A church was built over her grave.

UNKNOWN LaROSE[18]

She was a French woman who was buried on September 9, 1796 in Kingston, Frontenac, Upper Canada, British Colonial America. A church was built over her grave.

ELIAS LAKE[19]

Elias was buried on March 9, 1801 in Kingston, Frontenac, Upper Canada, British Colonial America. A church was built over his grave.

EDWARD WILLIAM LAMOINE[20]

Edward was buried on October 27, 1794 In Kingston, Frontenac, Upper Canada, British Colonial America. A church was built over his grave.

SUSAN (JOHNSON) LAMOINE[21]

Susan was born in 1772 in Johnstown, New York.

She was two years old when her father passed away in 1774.

Susan was five years old when her brother, Peter Warren, passed away in 1777.

Susan was 17 years old when she married Henry Lamoine in Rome, New York in 1789.

She was 22 years old when her son, Edward William, passed away in 1794. Her sister, Elizabeth, passed away on January 24th.

Susan was 23 years old when her husband passed away in 1795.

She was 24 years old when she passed away on December 28, 1795. Susan was buried on the 29th. A church was built over her grave.

PHILIP P. LANSINGH[22]

Philip was buried on November 6, 1792 in Kingston, Frontenac, Upper Canada, British Colonial America. A church was built over his grave.

FRANCIS LaPLANT[23]

F rancis was a sailor.

Hewas buried on August 23, 1802 in Kingston, Frontenac, Upper Canada, British Colonial America. A church was built over his grave.

JAMES LATHAM[24]

James was buried on June 30, 1799 in Kingston, Frontenac, Upper Canada, British Colonial America. A church was built over his grave.

MARY LAWSON[25]

Mary was buried on September 20, 1791 in Kingston, Frontenac, Upper Canada, British Colonial America. A church was built over her grave.

JOSEPH LEMOINE[26]

Joseph was born on August 14, 1795.

He was 18 years old when he passed away on July 2, 1814 in Kingston, Frontenac, Upper Canada, British Colonial America. A church was built over his grave.

PETER LENEY[27]

Peter was buried on January 6, 1806 in Kingston, Frontenac, Upper Canada, British Colonial America. A church was built over his grave.

UNKNOWN LINES[28]

She was married when she was buried on July 1, 1808. A church was built over her grave.

UNKNOWN LYNES[29]

They were a servant of Mr. Lynes before they passed away in 1794. A church was built over the grave.

MARGARET LYNES[30]

Margaret was buried on March 1, 1808 in Kingston, Frontenac, Upper Canada, British Colonial America. A church was built over her grave.

ANN (KIRBY) MACAULAY[31]

Ann was born in England in November 1770.

She was 20 years old when she married Robert Macaulay on February 13, 1791.

Ann was 29 years old when her husband passed away in 1800.

She was 30 years old when The Act of Union was passed in 1801.

Ann was 52 years old when her son, Robert, passed away in 1823.

She was 72 years old when "A Christmas Carol" was first published in 1843.

Ann was 79 years old when she passed away on January 20, 1850.

ROBERT MACAULAY[32]

Robert was born in 1796.

He was four years old when his father passed away in 1800.

Robert was a barrister when he passed away at the age of 27 on February 7, 1823. A church was built over his grave.

ROBERT MACAULAY[33]

Robert was born in Kingston, New York in 1744.

He was 47 years old when the first parliament of Upper Canada assembled on September 17, 1791. Robert married Ann on February 13th.

Robert was 56 years old when he passed away on September 2, 1800.

LT. WILLIAM MacKAY[34]

Wiilliam passed away in March 1801 and was buried in Kingston, Frontenac, Upper Canada, British Colonial America. A church was built over his grave.

MARY REBECCA MACKENZIE[35]

Mary passed away on November 6, 1816 and was buried in Kingston, Frontenac, Upper Canada, British Colonial America.

HARRIET McLEAN[36]

Harriet passed away in 1826 and was buried in Kingston, Frontenac, Upper Canada, British Colonial America. A church was built over her grave.

UNKNOWN MacMANN[37]

They were buried on January 8, 1792 in Kingston, Upper Canada, British Colonial America. A church was built over their grave.

ANNA (AIRD) MARKLAND[38]

Anna was born on March 9, 1788 in Montreal, Quebec.

She was 18 years old when her father passed away in 1806.

Anna was 20 years old when her sister, Martha, passed away in 1808.

She was 23 years old when she married in 1812. Her sister, Janet, passed away on January 30th.

Anna was 35 years old when her brother, John, passed away in 1823.

She was 44 years old when her sister, Rosina, passed away in 1832.

Anna was 45 years old when her brother, Findley, passed away in 1833.

She was 59 years old when she passed away on May 27, 1847.

THOMAS MARKLAND[39]

Thomas was born in 1757.

He was 34 years old when the first parliament of Upper Canada assembled on September 17, 1791.

Thomas was 83 years old when he passed away on January 31, 1840.

SILAS MAY[40]

Silas was born on February 18, 1789. He was christened on May 3rd in Conway, Massachusetts.

He was 22 years old when the War of 1812 took place. Silas married Mary Sloan on January 2, 1812.

Silas was 26 years old when his daughter, Susan, passed away in 1815.

He was 29 years old when he passed away on September 1, 1818. A church was built over his grave.

CHARLES McARTHUR[41]

Charles passed away in 1819 and was buried in Kingston, Frontenac, Upper Canada, British Colonial America. A church was built over his grave.

UNKNOWN McCARTY[42]

She was buried on September 17, 1793 in Kingston, Frontenac, Upper Canada, British Colonial America. A church was built over her grave.

JOHN McCRACKEN[43]

John passed away in 1813. A church was built over his grave.

CHARLES McCULLOCH[44]

Charles was buried on September 9, 1795 in Kingston, Frontenac, Upper Canada, British Colonial America. A church was built over his grave.

MARY McCURDY[45]

Mary passed away in 1813 and was buried in Kingston, Frontenac, Upper Canada, British Colonial America. A church was built over her grave.

UNKNOWN McDONALD[46]

She was married when she was buried on January 17, 1793 in Kingston, Frontenac, Upper Canada, British Colonial America. A church was built over her grave.

CHARLES McDONALD[47]

Charles passed away in 1815. A church was built over his grave.

UNKNOWN McDONNELL[48]

They were still a child when they were buried on January 3, 1794 in Kingston, Frontenac, Upper Canada, British Colonial America. A church was built over the grave.

ALEXANDER McDONNELL[49]

Alexander was buried on December 9, 1807 in Kingston, Frontenac, Upper Canada, British Colonial America. A church was built over his grave.

ALEXANDER McDONNELL [50]

Alexander was buried on February 15, 1794 in Kingston, Frontenac, Upper Canada, British Colonial America. A church was built over his grave.

CATHERINE McDONNELL[51]

Catherine was buried on April 8, 1799 in Kingston, Frontenac, Upper Canada, British Colonial America. A church was built over her grave.

DONALD McDONNELL[52]

Donald was buried on September 28, 1805 in Kingston, Frontenac, Upper Canada, British Colonial America. A church was built over his grave.

ELIZABETH McDONNELL[53]

Elizabeth was buried on April 12, 1805 in Kingston, Frontenac, Upper Canada, British Colonial America. A church was built over her grave.

JOHN McDONNELL [54]

John was buried on January 9, 1805 in Kingston, Frontenac, Upper Canada, British Colonial America. A church was built over his grave.

JOHN McDONNELL[55]

John was buried on July 3, 1802 in Kingston, Frontenac, Upper Canada, British Colonial America. A church was built over his grave.

WILLIAM McDONNELL[56]

William was buried on May 29, 1806 in Kingston, Frontenac, Upper Canada, British Colonial America. A church was built over his grave.

ELIZA McGOWAN[57]

Eliza was born in 1809.

She was 31 years old when she passed away on November 2, 1840.

ELIZA McGOWAN[58]

Eliza was born on October 29, 1840. Her mother passed away a few days later on November 2nd.

She was seven months old when she passed away on May 8, 1841.

LUCINDA McGOWAN[59]

Lucinda was born in 1809.

She was her husband's second wife.

Lucinda was 36 years old when she passed away on September 4, 1845.

SAMUEL McGOWAN, ESQ.[60]

Samuel was born in Londonderry, Ireland in 1790.

He was eight years old when the Battle of Antrim took place in 1798. That same year the Young Ireland rebellion failed.

Samuel was 50 years old when his wife, Eliza, passed away followed by his daughter Eliza when he was 51.

He was 55 years old when his second wife, Lucinda, passed away in 1845.

Samuel was 57 years old when he passed away on October 29, 1847.

JOHN McGUIRE[61]

John was buried on October 20, 1805 in Kingston, Frontenac, Upper Canada, British Colonial America. A church was built over his grave.

UNKNOWN McINTYRE[62]

They were only a child when they were buried on August 17, 1803. A church was built over their grave.

J. D. McKAY[63]

They were buried on October 11, 1799.
A church was built over their grave.

ROBERT McKAY[64]

Robert was buried on January 1, 1807.
A church was built over his grave.

UNKNOWN McLAUGHLIN[65]

They were buried on September 19, 1794.
A church was built over the grave.

UNKNOWN McLAUGHLIN[66]

She was married when she was buried on March 18, 1808. A church was built over her grave.

UNKNOWN McLEAN[67]

He passed away in 1824.
A church was built over his grave.

MARY McLEAN[68]

Mary passed away in 1815.
A church was built over her grave.

NEIL McLEAN[69]

Neil was buried on September 1, 1795.
A church was built over his grave.

JOHN McLEOD [70]

John was buried on April 1, 1800.
A church was built over his grave.

JOHN McMULLEN[71]

John passed away on December 23, 1801.
A church was built over his grave.

JOHN McQUINN[72]

John served in the 100th Regiment.
He passed away in August 1809.
A church was built over his grave.

DAVID McWILLIAMS[73]

David was buried on June 8, 1809.
A church was built over his grave.

MARY A. MENDS[74]

Mary passed away in 1821.
A church was built over her grave.

HENRY MERCY[75]

Henry was buried on July 28, 1808.
A church was built over his grave.

GEORGE MERRILL [76]

George passed away in 1823.
A church was built over his grave.

MARY MERRILS[77]

Mary was buried on July 11, 1803.
A church was built over her grave.

SARAH MERRILS[78]

Sarah was buried on February 24, 1805.
A church was built over her grave.

JOSEPH MERRIT[79]

Joseph was buried on April 29, 1792.
A church was built over his grave.

ELIZABETH METCALF[80]

Elizabeth was born in 1800.

She was 41 years old when she passed away on April 21, 1841. A church was built over her grave.

MARGARET (SOADEN) METCALF[81]

Margaret was born in 1803.

She was John Metcalf's second wife.

Margaret was 41 years old when she passed away in 1844. A church was built over her grave.

AL AND DOLLY MEURLING[82]

(N*o dates are currently available. Please see the footnote.*)

REV. MYERS[83]

He was buried on October 17, 1793.
A church was built over his grave.

JANE (EARL) MILLER[84]

Jane was born in 1809.

She was three years old when the War of 1812 took place. Jane was nine years old when her mother passed away in 1818. She was 54 years old when she passed away on March 25, 1863.

CATHERINE SOPHIA (BAGG) MILLS[85]

Catherine was born on July 4, 1850 in Montreal, Quebec.

She was 16 years old when Ontario was founded on July 1, 1867.

Catherine was 62 years old when the Central Banking System was established in 1913.

She was 83 years old when the Dionne Quintuplets were born in 1934.

Catherine was 86 years old when the Neutrality Act was passed in 1937.

She was 87 years old when she passed away in 1938.

A church was built over her grave.

# WILLIAM LENNOX MILLS[86]

William was born on January 27, 1846 in Woodstock, Brock, Canada West, British Colonial America.

He was 20 years old when Ontario was founded on July 1, 1867.

William was 71 years old when he passed away on May 4, 1917. A church was built over his grave.

ELIZABETH MILTON[87]

ELIZABETH WAS BURIED on April 23, 1796.
A church was built over her grave.

THOMAS MILTON[88]

Thomas was buried on May 17, 1807.
A church was built over his grave.

JOHN MININGER[89]

John was buried on April 11, 1795.
A church was built over his grave.

WILLIAM MITCHELL[90]

William passed away in 1820.
A church was built over his grave.

UNKNOWN MORRILL[91]

He passed away in 1812.
A church was built over his grave.

MARGARET MORRISON[92]

Margaret was buried on August 28, 1805. A church was built over her grave.

ELIZA MALLORY MOSIER[93]

Eliza passed away in 1816.
A church was built over her grave.

UNKNOWN MUIR[94]

They were only a child when they were buried on July 21, 1792. A church was built over the grave.

UNKNOWN MUIRHEAD[95]

She was married when she was buried on January 3, 1793.
A church was built over her grave.

CHARLES SMYTH MURNEY[96]

Charles was born in 1803 in Kingston, Frontenac, Upper Canada, British Colonial America.

He was less than a year old when his brother, Edward, passed away in 1804.

Charles was five years old when his brother, Henry Chambers, passed away in 1809.

He was eight years old when he passed away on January 4, 1812. A church was built over his grave.

HENRY CHAMBERS MURNEY[97]

Henry was born in 1807.

He was a year old when he was buried on March 27, 1809. A church was built over his grave.

HENRY MURNEY[98]

Henry passed away in 1816.
A church was built over his grave.

CAPTAIN HENRY JAMES MURNEY[99]

Henry was born in 1759.

He was 43 years old when his wife passed away in 1802. He married Catherine Smyth on July 5th.

Henry was 45 years old when his son, Edward, passed away in 1804.

He was 50 years old when his son, Henry Chambers, passed away in 1809.

Henry was 53 years old when his son, Charles Smyth, passed away in 1812.

He was 73 years old when his son, William Frend Murney, Esq., passed away in 1832.

Henry was 76 years old when he passed away on August 13, 1835.

WILLIAM FRIEND MURNEY, ESQ. [100]

William was born in 1809.

He was less than a year old when his brother, Henry Chambers, passed away in 1809.

William was three years old when his brother, Charles Smyth, passed away in 1812.

He was 23 years old and a barrister when he passed away on June 6, 1832. A church was built over his grave.

ANN NORTON[101]

Ann passed away in 1818.
A church was built over her grave.

LOOMIS NORTON[102]

L oomis passed away in 1824.
 A church was built over his grave.

[1] https://www.wikitree.com/genealogy/Jackson-Family-Tree-51371

[2] https://www.wikitree.com/genealogy/James-Family-Tree-25518

[3] https://www.wikitree.com/genealogy/Jelley-Family-Tree-682

[4] https://www.wikitree.com/genealogy/Johnson-Family-Tree-126775

[5] https://www.wikitree.com/genealogy/Brant-Family-Tree-317

[6] https://www.wikitree.com/genealogy/Johnson-Family-Tree-122259

[7] https://www.wikitree.com/genealogy/Johnson-Family-Tree-126778

[8] https://www.wikitree.com/genealogy/Jones-Family-Tree-124449

[9] https://www.wikitree.com/genealogy/Jones-Family-Tree-124467

[10] https://www.wikitree.com/genealogy/Stuart-Family-Tree-430

[11] https://www.wikitree.com/genealogy/Jones-Family-Tree-124470

[12] https://www.wikitree.com/genealogy/Kantz-Family-Tree-72

[13] https://www.wikitree.com/genealogy/Kayton-Family-Tree-24

[14] https://www.wikitree.com/genealogy/Keith-Family-Tree-6666

[15] https://www.wikitree.com/genealogy/Killaly-Family-Tree-7

[16] https://www.wikitree.com/genealogy/Kindle-Family-Tree-325

[17] https://www.wikitree.com/genealogy/Kirby-Family-Tree-7604

[18] https://www.wikitree.com/genealogy/LaRose-Family-Tree-719

[19] https://www.wikitree.com/genealogy/Lake-Family-Tree-5858

[20] https://www.wikitree.com/genealogy/Lamoine-Family-Tree-15

[21] https://www.wikitree.com/genealogy/Johnson-Family-Tree-122253

[22] https://www.wikitree.com/genealogy/Lansingh-Family-Tree-5

[23] https://www.wikitree.com/genealogy/LaPlant-Family-Tree-233

[24] https://www.wikitree.com/genealogy/Latham-Family-Tree-3906

[25] https://www.wikitree.com/genealogy/Lawson-Family-Tree-12320

[26] https://www.wikitree.com/genealogy/Lemoine-Family-Tree-1011

[27] https://www.wikitree.com/genealogy/Leney-Family-Tree-185

[28] https://www.wikitree.com/genealogy/Lines-Family-Tree-1232

[29] https://www.wikitree.com/genealogy/Lynes-Family-Tree-268

[30] https://www.wikitree.com/genealogy/Lynes-Family-Tree-269

[31] https://www.wikitree.com/genealogy/Kirby-Family-Tree-2188

[32] https://www.wikitree.com/genealogy/Macaulay-Family-Tree-97

[33] https://www.wikitree.com/genealogy/Macaulay-Family-Tree-94

[34] https://www.wikitree.com/genealogy/MacKay-Family-Tree-5436

[35] https://www.wikitree.com/genealogy/Mackenzie-Family-Tree-6497

[36] https://www.wikitree.com/genealogy/McLean-Family-Tree-10604

[37] https://www.wikitree.com/genealogy/MacMann-Family-Tree-7

[38] https://www.wikitree.com/genealogy/Aird-Family-Tree-558

[39] https://www.wikitree.com/genealogy/Markland-Family-Tree-325

[40] https://www.wikitree.com/genealogy/May-Family-Tree-14744

[41] https://www.wikitree.com/genealogy/McArthur-Family-Tree-3188

[42] https://www.wikitree.com/genealogy/Unknown-Family-Tree-618161

[43] https://www.wikitree.com/genealogy/McCracken-Family-Tree-4215

[44] https://www.wikitree.com/genealogy/McCulloch-Family-Tree-2441

[45] https://www.wikitree.com/genealogy/McCurdy-Family-Tree-1991

[46] https://www.wikitree.com/genealogy/Unknown-Family-Tree-618164

[47] https://www.wikitree.com/genealogy/McDonald-Family-Tree-27162

[48] https://www.wikitree.com/genealogy/McDonnell-Family-Tree-2092

[49] https://www.wikitree.com/genealogy/McDonnell-Family-Tree-2093

[50] https://www.wikitree.com/genealogy/McDonnell-Family-Tree-2094

[51] https://www.wikitree.com/genealogy/McDonnell-Family-Tree-2095

[52] https://www.wikitree.com/genealogy/McDonnell-Family-Tree-2096

[53] https://www.wikitree.com/genealogy/McDonnell-Family-Tree-2097

[54] https://www.wikitree.com/genealogy/McDonnell-Family-Tree-2098

[55] https://www.wikitree.com/genealogy/McDonnell-Family-Tree-2099

[56] https://www.wikitree.com/genealogy/McDonnell-Family-Tree-2100

[57] https://www.wikitree.com/genealogy/Unknown-Family-Tree-590466

[58] https://www.wikitree.com/genealogy/McGowan-Family-Tree-3515

[59] https://www.wikitree.com/genealogy/McGowan-Family-Tree-3513

[60] https://www.wikitree.com/genealogy/McGowan-Family-Tree-3514

[61] https://www.wikitree.com/genealogy/McGuire-Family-Tree-6825

[62] https://www.wikitree.com/genealogy/McIntyre-Family-Tree-7036

[63] https://www.wikitree.com/genealogy/McKay-Family-Tree-8753

[64] https://www.wikitree.com/genealogy/McKay-Family-Tree-8938

[65] https://www.wikitree.com/genealogy/McLaughlin-Family-Tree-8076

[66] https://www.wikitree.com/genealogy/Unknown-Family-Tree-618206

[67] https://www.findagrave.com/memorial/175050290/mclean

[68] https://www.wikitree.com/genealogy/McLean-Family-Tree-10607

[69] https://www.wikitree.com/genealogy/McLean-Family-Tree-10609

[70] https://www.wikitree.com/genealogy/McLeod-Family-Tree-8165

[71] https://www.wikitree.com/genealogy/McMullen-Family-Tree-2643

[72] https://www.wikitree.com/genealogy/McQuin-Family-Tree-61

[73] https://www.wikitree.com/genealogy/McWilliams-Family-Tree-2208

[74] https://www.wikitree.com/genealogy/Mends-Family-Tree-9

[75] https://www.wikitree.com/genealogy/Mercy-Family-Tree-73

[76] https://www.wikitree.com/genealogy/Merrill-Family-Tree-6108

[77] https://www.wikitree.com/genealogy/Merrils-Family-Tree-7

[78] https://www.wikitree.com/genealogy/Merrils-Family-Tree-8

[79] https://www.wikitree.com/genealogy/Merrit-Family-Tree-168

[80] https://www.wikitree.com/genealogy/Unknown-Family-Tree-618224

[81] https://www.wikitree.com/genealogy/Soaden-Family-Tree-1

[82] https://www.findagrave.com/memorial/194248255/al_and_dolly-meurling

[83] https://www.wikitree.com/genealogy/Myers-Family-Tree-21772

[84] https://www.wikitree.com/genealogy/Earl-Family-Tree-1807

[85] https://www.wikitree.com/genealogy/Bagg-Family-Tree-359

[86] https://www.wikitree.com/genealogy/Mills-Family-Tree-25047

[87] https://www.wikitree.com/genealogy/Milton-Family-Tree-2197

[88] https://www.wikitree.com/genealogy/Milton-Family-Tree-2198

[89] https://www.wikitree.com/genealogy/Mininger-Family-Tree-16

[90] https://www.wikitree.com/genealogy/Mitchell-Family-Tree-39865

[91] https://www.wikitree.com/genealogy/Morrill-Family-Tree-1582

[92] https://www.wikitree.com/genealogy/Morrison-Family-Tree-18584

[93] https://www.wikitree.com/genealogy/Mosler-Family-Tree-879

[94] https://www.wikitree.com/genealogy/Muir-Family-Tree-4646

[95] https://www.wikitree.com/genealogy/Unknown-Family-Tree-618276

[96] https://www.wikitree.com/genealogy/Murney-Family-Tree-44

[97] https://www.wikitree.com/genealogy/Murney-Family-Tree-45

[98] https://www.wikitree.com/genealogy/Murney-Family-Tree-46

[99] https://www.wikitree.com/genealogy/Murney-Family-Tree-14

[100] https://www.wikitree.com/genealogy/Murney-Family-Tree-47

[101] https://www.wikitree.com/genealogy/Norton-Family-Tree-11068

[102] https://www.wikitree.com/genealogy/Norton-Family-Tree-11069

Don't miss out!

Visit the website below and you can sign up to receive emails whenever Angeline Gallant publishes a new book. There's no charge and no obligation.

https://books2read.com/r/B-A-QGSI-LFCBC

Also by Angeline Gallant

A Dragon's Diary
Dreaming of Dragons

Blood and Spirit Saga
The Rising Wind

Calling Her Heart
Whisper of the Heart
Calling Her Heart Volumes 1 & 2: A Small Town Romance
Collection
No Turning Back
Calling Her Heart volumes 3 & 4
Forsake Me Not
Hear My Cry

FORGET ME NOT
Victoria, Ontario's Babies 1894 - 1895

Guardian of the Heart
Fallen Petals

Keeper Of Secrets
A Lady's Secret

Kingston's Love Chronicles
Springtime Promises

Midnight's Awakening
Heart of the Storm
Walking Through The Storm
Walking Through The Storm
Fighting the Storm
Call Me Cursed
Heart of the Storm

Secrets of the Underworld
Deklan's Dragons

Tell My Story Collection
Tell My Story: Germany 1851
Tell My Story: England 1852

Whispers From The Garrison Church

The Dervock Legacy
Echoes of Dervock

The Grave Whisperer
German Prisoners of War in Canada
Cataraqui United Church Cemetery
Whispers of Kingston
Wedding Bells in Kingston, Ontario, Canada 1923
St. Paul's Anglican Churchyard A-B
St. Paul's Anglican Churchyard C-D
St. Paul's Anglican Churchyard E - F
St. Paul's Anglican Churchyard, Kingston, Ontario, Canada G - H
St. Paul's Anglican Churchyard J - N
St. Paul's Anglican Churchyard, Kingston, Ontario, Canada O - R
St. Paul's Anglican Churchyard, Kingston, Ontario, Canada S - T
St. Paul's Anglican Churchyard, Kingston, Ontario T - Z
Small Graveyards & Burial Grounds: Kingston, Ontario, Canada
Cataraqui United Church Cemetery 1
Cataraqui United Church Cemetery 2
Cataraqui United Church Cemetary 3
Cataraqui United Church Cemetery 4
Cataraqui United Church Cemetery 5
Beth Israel Cemetery
Cataraqui United Church Cemetery 6
Beneath the Surface: Echoes from Beth Israel Cemetery
Grave Tales: Discovering the Lives of Beth Israel
Whispers Beneath St. Paul's

The Timeless Veil
Eternal Devotion

The Wolf Whisperer Series
Captured Heart
Fate's Legacy
Mohawk Valley
Cry of a Warrior
Wolf Whisperer volumes 1 & 2
Endless White
The Wolf Whisperer volumes 1 & 2

Timeless
The Time Keeper's Sanctuary

Timeless Whispers of Dervock Saga
Secrets of Dervock

Standalone
Winds of Change vol 1-3

About the Author

Angeline Gallant traces her roots through generations of Old Stock Canadian heritage, her passion for genealogy as deep and enduring as the forests and fields her ancestors once walked. With a reverence for history and an eye for detail, she weaves stories from the fragments of lives left behind in letters, records, and weathered headstones.

An avid reader and devoted writer, Angeline brings the past to life with a curiosity for heraldry and a deep love for the landscapes that shaped her family's story. Each name and date she uncovers feels less like history and more like coming home, a familiar echo in the vast tapestry of time. For her, these stories are not forgotten—they live, breathing in the quiet spaces of memory and tradition, a testament to lives once lived, now eternal in the pages of her books.

Read more at https://www.goodreads.com/author/show/19703964.Angeline_Gallant.

www.ingramcontent.com/pod-product-compliance
Lightning Source LLC
Chambersburg PA
CBHW071525150726

48000CB00002B/688